Ernest Hemingway
For Whom The Bell Tolls

A.A. Khan

ADHYAYAN

ADHYAYAN PUBLISHERS & DISTRIBUTORS
New Delhi-110002

Published by
ADHYAYAN PUBLISHERS & DISTRIBUTORS
4378/4B, 105, J.M.D. House, Murari Lal Street
Ansari Road Darya Ganj, New Delhi - 110002
Ph.: 011-23263018, 011-23277156, Fax: 011-23262856
Email: adhyayanpublishers@yahoo.com

Ernest Hemingway For Whom The Bell Tolls

Edition 2013

ISBN 978-81-8435-386-0

PRINTED IN INDIA

Published by Harish Chandra Yadav for Adhyayan Publishers & Distributors, Delhi. Printed at Tarun Offset Printer, Delhi.

Preface

Hemingway's *For Whom The Bell Tolls* appeared in 1940 when the Second World War was on. The aim of the Allied Powers was to fight war to end war. Years before, Ernest Hemingway on seeing the miseries of refugees in Graeco-Turkish War decided to be a writer to prevent wars. *For Whom The Bell Tolls* rouses the conscience of humanity against oppressions and atrocities resulting in ward.

The study of *For Whom The Bell Tolls* has relevance for all times to come. It is not merley a "one-visit book," to Spain. Hemingway's involvement in the Spanish Civil War is the tragedy of humanity. Hence the enduring appeal of *For Whom The Bell Tolls.*

In the first chapter, I have discussed Hemingway's cosmopolitan approach. Europe was his school, Paris his home and Spain his love. I have discussed the economic, political and religious causes of the Spanish Civil War. Ernest Hemingway's involvement in the Spanish Civil War was the result of his love for the oppressed humanity.

In the second chapter, I have discussed Hemingway's method of narration. The choice of the title from John Donne's Meditation 17, is significant and highly suggestive of the theme. Ernest Hemingway is a highly implicative writer. So, Hemingway's artistic use of symbolism and irony has been critically examined with particular reference to the novel.

The third chapter deals with Robert Jordan, the hero of the novel. Robert Jordan, the physically and mentally wounded hero shown gradual change from gloomy despair to sunny hope and faith. Robert Jordan is not a code hero like Wilson, but a "Hemingway Hero," not having a code to follow.

In the fourth chapter, I have discussed important characters of Maria, Pablo, Pilar and Anselmo. Through these characters Hemingway convinces us that war is a bad thing.

In the fifth chapter I have discussed the place of *For Whom The Bell Tolls* in literature. The novel shows Hemingway's sympathy for anti-Fascist movement. Moreover, Robert Jordan shows grace under pressure which is expressive of his moral courage. His advice to Pablo "to use his head," is expressive of his desire to awaken the conscience of humanity against tyranny and oppression. I have discussed the typical Hemingway style which has found many imitators but no true successors. The Novel Prize Citation has rightly pointed out that Hemingway is one of the moulders of the modern style of writing.

In the end, I have given a glossary of the Spanish words and phrases used in the novel.

A.A. Khan

Contents

BOOKS AUTHORED/EDITED

By
Professor A.A. Khan

1. Layers of Violence—*The Novels of George Orwell*
2. George Orwell— *The Way to Nineteen Eighty Four*
3. A Holistic Approach to Communication
4. Ruth Prawer Jhabvala's Fiction—*Existential Modes and Stylistic Patterns*
5. Jayanta Mahapatra—*His Mind and Art*
6. Ernest Hemingway—*Short Stories and Humanism*
7. Nissim Ezekiel—*Poetry as Social Criticism*
8. Changing Faces of New Woman Indian Writing in English
9. Grooming The Middle—*Life and Perspective in the Novels of E.M. Forster*
10. Emergence of New Woman— *Indian Writing in English*
11. English Language Teaching—*A Socio-Functional View*
12. The Eternal Woman—*Indian Writing in English*
13. Ernest Hemingway—*For Whom The Bell Tolls*

1

Introduction

Ernest Hemingway died of self-inflicted gunshot wound on July 2, 1961. The gunshot, so to say, was heard all over the world. The obituaries were published in all the papers of the world. It is a strange co-incidence that his father . Dr. Edmonds Hemingway, also ended his life by committing suicide, Ernest Hemingway kept the gun with him as a historical keep sake.

Ernest Hemingway grew up in a repressed atmosphere at home, where the parents had exchanged their traditional roles. It was fortunate that cooking was Dr. Hemingway's hobby, Ernest's mother, Grace, was not interested in house", keeping Ernest Hemingway said about his mother that she was a music nut and a frustrated singer. In later life, Ernest had always admiration for those women. Who were good cooks. In For Whom The Ben Tolls, Maria is also a good cook:

> The girl Maria can cook a little..... she
> cooks well to please her. But mostly she helps
> The mujer of Pablo.

The repressed atmosphere played. an important role in moulding his attitudes reflecting the homelessness of his heroes.

Hemingway's Cosmopolitan Approach

Soon after high school, Ernest securing in securing a job as ambulance driver at the Italian Front.. Within one week he was seriously wounded while carrying a wounded soldier to a red cross post. When surrounded with dead and dying he felt it natural to die than to go on living. It was this incident which developed him into something larger and bigger. After being discharged from the hospital, Ernest came to his native place, America could not hold him long. He came to Paris, the paradise of expatriates. He came in contact with Gertrude Stem. The spectacle of refugee misery which he saw in October, 1922, left a permanent scar on him. He decided "cold as a snake" to be a writer and to write as truly as he could. "Ernest Hemingway's college and gradus ad parnansum was the continent of Europe." Ernest met Ezra Pound. "To Miss Stem, he seemed an extraordinarily handsome youngman, with an air more continental than American ..." Ezra Pound recognized Hemingway's abilities. John Peale Bishop reached Paris in. 1922. He asked Ezra Pound who were the ablest American expatriates living in Paris. Ezra Pound took him to Hemingway. Bishop was impressed. Ernest's integrity could be trusted completely. He could not be bought. Hemingway was a perpetual student, the omnivorous reader, the brilliant naturalist and the curious questioner. Ernest Hemingway made the artistic use of his Paris experiences during the writing of *For Whom The Bell Tolls* in 1939-40.

Hemingway's Love for Spain

Spain is an important country in the South-West of Europe. In Spanish language the country is called. Espans, the Arabs called it Hisponia. Spain and her people have very strong and marked characteristic. The Spaniards have been known for their adventurous spirit. As a result of it the Spaniards have been responsible for great achievements. America was discovered by Columbus on October 12, 1492,

The Spaniards take delight in bloody sports like bull fighting. To a superficial reader, bull-fighting may appear a cruel and in human game. Ernest Hemingway has written the book Death in *The Afternoon* dealing with bull fighting. It is an important non-fiction work of Hemingway. Its value lies in interpreting the aesthetic principles of bull fighting. Ernest Hemingway has narrated the incident of an old lady who could not stand the sight of bull fight it is a common experience that many of the first visitors in barrera (the ring round the arena in bull fighting), scream with honour when they see the animal of the matador being gored to death. Ernest Hemingway was the lower of wild big games. Once he took his friends to task because they could not stand the sight of a carriage carrying decomposed corpses of the dogs. He labeled his friends as "romantics." A bull-fighter is called a matador in Spanish language. A matador is different from a butcher. A matador has courage, dignity, control on nerves, swiftness and precision. There are rules of bull-fighting. The matador has a high code of conduct. The Spanish word *Pudnor* courage and probity. The festivities of Fiesta begin with fire works and continues through a noisy week of drinking and dancing with religious *processions and special Masses in the churches and bull-fights every afternoon..* The Spaniards love to flirt with death in bull-fighting. In 1923, when Ernest visited Spain, five of the best matadors were gored to death in the first-five days of the Fiesta celebrations. Ernest was interested in bull-fighting. He had intimate friendship with the famous bull fighters of the time. He was great admirer of the matador Manuel Garcia called Meera:

> By God, write Ernest, have bull fights in that town. The vilar bulls were fast and brave, with horns like sword blades. Among the matadors, he singled out two for special attention. One was Nicanor Villalta, a native of Aragon ... The other was Manuel Carcia, called Meera
>
> ... He loved. to kill bulls and lived. with much passion and enjoyment Ernest and Hadley agreed that if they had a son they would name him for Nicanor Villalta. But it was to Mera, Ernest paid the highest tribute he could think of Eramuy, 'Eramuy hombre'.

Ernest Hemingway does not regard bull-fighting merely as a wild sport. He had a high regard for bull-fighters, who by their precision skill, became artist in their act of killing bulls. The final killing of bull is called the "moment of truth." *In The Sun Also Rises*, Ernest Hemingway says about bull-fighters "Nobody ever lives their life all the way up except bull-fighters."

Ernest loved bull-fighting as much that once he told Scott that "my idea of heaven was a bull-ring where I had the permanent seat, with a rushing—trout stream. outside that could be fished by me and my pal. ..."

The Spanish Civil War

For Whom The Bell Tolls was first published in 1940. It deals with the Spanish Civil. "War, which ended in 1939. It was an important political event affecting the whole of the continent. The Second World War which began in 1939, over-shadowed the Spanish Civil War. Ernest Hemingway had closely observed the political developments of Spain. On seeing the political situation of Spain, Ernest Hemingway predicted that the Second Ward War was no far off and his prediction came true. *For Whom The Bell Tolls* deals with the Spanish Civil War. So, it is significant to note that the important events of the Spanish Civil War. The civil wars are of native origin. As the name suggests, it is an armed conflict within the country. The country itself is divided into two groups bent upon smashing the other in the armed conflict. History bears witness to the fact that the civil war in a country is the result of simmering and see thing discontent. Of course, a minor incident sparks off the civil war. So it happened with the Spanish Civil War. There was also foreign intervention in the Spanish Civil war from almost all the European countries.

Political Causes

The Spanish monarchy had been the uniting force between the diverse regions of Spain. The Bolshevic Revolution in

Russia brought about the end of the Czar monarchy. It spread like a contagion and different monarchs felt tremors under their shaky thrones. Spain could not escape the contagion and anti-monarchist sentiments became evident in the form of strikes and disturbances. These strikes and disturbances were crushed by the Spanish army in 1920. In 1923, the army again came to the rescue of the Spanish monarchy. The army succeeded in crushing the disturbances, but at the same time it gave warning to King Alfanso III that it might stay aloof if such occasion comes again. There was growing unpopularity of monarchy. The army was gradually becoming weak. The leftist movement gained momentum. The municipal elections were held in 1931, in which the polls were swept by the leftists. King Alfanso III went into voluntary exile. Spain become a Republic in 1931. There was a series of bloody strikes in 1934. There was growing dissatisfaction against the ruling class of the land owners, the aristocracy and the church. At one time about 700 Ovitio miners were shot by the army.

Religious Causes

The Catholic Church of Spain was more powerful than the monarchy and more pervasive than the army. The church owned industries, banks, schools, in the press and about one-third of the total wealth of the nation. The church was against the republic because it meant an end of its powers. The church was dead against the Marxist Atheism because it threatened Christianity itself So, the church joined hands with Fascists and Royalists to fight against the labourers. The common people went against the church. They made the churches, priests and nuns their first targets. In *For Whom the Bell Tolls,* Pilar says about Pablo that he hated priests even worse than he hated Fascists. "To many religious observers the civil war appeared to be a holy war in which the Nationalists were the crusaders fighting against the forces of evil. This Francisco Franco, the Spanish General, drew a great deal of sympathy in waging a war against the so called destroyers of religions."

Economics Causes

The economic structure was feudal. The Spanish economy was backward.. The majority of people depended on land for their livelihood. Most of them lived on the verge of starvation. The ownerships of land was in the hands of a few feudal Lords. The labourers in industries were in equally bad condition. The world depression of 1920 badly hit the industries and landless farmers. The landless farmers and labourers found a ray of hope in republic. The labour unions created a feeling among the labourers that the cure for their poverty and starvation lay in the establishment of the Republic. The labourers and common people were satisfied when the Republic was formed on April 14, 1931. The land owners, the Church, the monarchy and the army opposed the reform measures of the Republicans. As a result, the Republicans failed to fulfill their promises. Strikes and labour unrest became common affairs. Political murders began to take place every day on both sides. The army began to oppose the government on July 17, 1936. The loyalist militia was formed by the government. But the army went ahead with a carefully worked out plan. The civil war had begun.

T'he Political Upheavals

After 1931, the Communist-Socialist coalition ruled Spain for two years. It was plagued by strikes and agitations. The general election was held in November, 1933. The rightists were returned to power with a large majority. The Conversatives remained in power for a little more two years. In January 1936, when general election was held, the public opinion had swung back to its previous position. The leftist won this election but will a smaller majority. After five months Jose Calvas Otelo was assassinated. The precipitated a revolt by the army General Fancisco Franco was called back. Franco quickly overthrew the government in Spanish Horocco. Within a few hours after Franco's arrival in Spain, his forces took several of the larger Spanish cities. However, the Government's Militia brought this initial surge to a temporary halt. The capital city Madrid remained in the hands of the Loyalist leftists. By August 1936 the foreign intervention became an accomplished fact. Russia was sending 'observers' and 'volunteers' Russia also sent financial and donated by its people to help· in the leftist cause. However, Russia was not industrially capable of giving a great deal of aid in the form of material. Germany and Italy sen planes, tanks and ammunitions in support of the rightists. By January 1939, Franco's troops began to collapse, Finally, on March 22, 1939, the Monarchist forces overcome the resistance of the besieged city of Madrid, The long and bitter civil war came to an end. The intervention was responsible for atrocities.

> International politics played a great part in the civil war during the next two years, giving the advantage first to one side and then to the other. Throughout this period both sides committed sickening' atrocities. The Loyalists were charged with the murders of hundreds of members of the elergy and well as the assassination of their political enemies and the systematic bombing and strafing of non-military objectives by the Monarchists was a portent of things to come in World War II.

The nature of the Spanish Civil was very complex: Neither of the sides drew whole hearted sympathy or condemnation. The people who believed in democracy sided with the Republicans but were hurt by their irreligious acts such as the burning of churches and killing of priests. The religious minded people felt it to be a holy war against evil.

Hemingway's Involvement

Hemingway was great admirer and lover of Spain, its people, its language and its sports. In many of his stories we found reference to Spain. The old fisherman in *The Old Man and The Sea* is called Santiago. In Spanish language

Santiago means a saint. Ernest Hemingway donated the Gold Medal of Nobel Prize to the shrine of Santiago. Hemingway's two short stories, "The Chauffeurs of Madrid" and "The Butterfly and The Tank" deal with the incidents connected with the Spanish Civil War. Hemingway's love for big game and wildlife hunting show his temperamental affinity with Spanish national character. His stories and novels are full of Spanish sentences. Ernest Hemingway's involvement in Spanish Civil War was the result of his genuine interest in the Spanish people. Ernest Hemingway felt relieved at the collapse of monarchy in Spain in 1931. At the same time he disapproved of the anti-clerical riots the same year. Politically he was also on the side of the Republic. Ernest Hemingway was known for his impartiality and objectivity. At first he did not want to go to Spain, but when the civil war started he could not resist the temptation of taking active interest in Spain. Hemingway paid for the passage of two volunteers going to join the Loyalists. He collected. 40,000 for ambulances and medical supplies. He worked with others on a documentary film, *Spain In Flames*. Ernest Hemingway's interest was on a humanitarian basis. Hemingway made four trips to Spain during the civil war. First trip was on February 27, 1937. He was a correspondent of the North American Newspaper Alliance (NANA). His aim was to collect dispassionate reports about the civil war. There had been already foreign intervention in the internal matters of Spain. Hemingway was an anti-war correspondent who wanted to keep America away from involving itself in the Spanish Civil War. During his first trip he spent forty-five days. On return to the United States of America, Ernest Hemingway was a confirmed anti-Fascist. He was confirmed in his opinion that Fascism cannot produce good writers. During his stay in Spain Ernest Hemingway helped Joris Ivens in making *The Spanish Earth,* a documentary film on the civil War Hemingway visited Spain second time on August 14, 1937. He stayed in Spanish up to January 28,

1948, He wrote the play *The Fifty Column.* In this play Hemingway adopted an objective and impartial attitude towards the civil was. It was sympathetic to the republic but did not dearly plead for the cause of the Loyalists. Hemingway's third visit was for twelve days from May 19 to May 31, 1938. He wrote articles asking the US Government to lift its embargo on the sale of arms to Spain, The fourth trip to Spain was from September 2, 1930 to the 'winter of that year. At the end of March 1939, Barcelona and Madrid. had fallen and. the civil war ended. *For Whom The Bell Talls* was written in 1939 and published in 1940. It deals with the Spanish Civil War but there is very little politics in it. Hemingway had used his articles and film for propaganda purposes. In this novel, *For Whom The Bell Tolls,* he maintains a careful balance. He did not allow his novels to become an instrument of propaganda for either side in the civil war. Like a true artist Hemingway turned his first hand experience of the civil war into a great work of art. Ernest Hemingway kept himself above any ideological affiliations.

Hemingway's deep understanding of the Spanish temperament is revealed in *For Whom The Bell Tolls.* Hemingways novel is altogether different from Julies Mier Grafe's *The Spanish Journey,* and Waldo *Frank's Virgin Spain,* These two books have lost their importance with the passage of time. But *For Whom The Bell Tolls* is a work of art. The little is highly suggestive of an individual involvement with the rest of humanity. The method of narration has an artistic charm. The artistic use of symbolism and irony makes clear the Iceberg principle operative in this novel.

2

The Narrative—The Method of Narration

Title

Ernest Hemingway derived the title from John Donne's Meditation 17. John Donne was a metaphysical poet of the seventeenth century. Ernest Hemingway was very meticulous about his titles. He derived the title of *In Out Turn* from common prayer Book. The title of a short story *In Another Country* is derived from Marlowe. *Winner Take Nothing* is derived from book of games. Ernest Hemingway has quoted the whole passage from Meditation 17 on the title page of the novel *For Whom The Bell Tolls:*

> No man is an Iland intire of it selfe; every may is a peece of the continent, a part of the maines; if a clod bee washed away by the sea, Europe is the lesse, as well as if a promontorie were, as well as if a Mannor of thy friends or of thine owne were any mans death diminishes me, because I am involved in Mankinde, And therefore never send to know for whom. the been tolls; it tolls for thee. John Donne (p. 3)

The sermon is definitely not optimistic in Donne's sense. Yet the sermon advises us to hand together to avoid hanging separately. We are not as lonely as we thought we are involved in mankind.

Donne's sermon conveys the theme of the novel. It is

interesting to note that T.S. Eliot began his *The Waste Land* with an epigraph of Sybil. The epigraph is part of the poem while Ernest Hemingway has not used John Donne's Meditation 17 as an epigraph. On the other hand Ernest Hemingway has written it just under the title of the novel on the front page. Ernest Hemingway produces an artistic effect by leaving many things unsaid. However, Ernest Hemingway was more an innovator than an imitator. Ernest Hemingway used John Donne's Meditation 17 in his own way. The epigraph on Sybil and Donne's quotations deal with death, but there is a vast difference between the two Sybil is fed up with her good-far-nothing life. Donne's Meditation 17 shows the inevitability of death, and at the Same time it shows the involvement of every man with the lot of whole mankind. Like Donne Hemingway believes on the oneness of mankind. Harry Morgan says that a man alone has no chance. He Subscribes to Donne's motto "No man is an Iland..... " Ernest Hemingway suggests that the human beings are essentially the same- Spanish or American fascists or loyalists. With the help of Donne's Meditation 17, Hemingway tells us that the human beings are inter-related by their mutual concern. And at the same time maintain their individuality. Robert Jordan is helping the Spanish people in their fight against the Fascists. If the bell tolls for Jordan, it tolls for every human being. John Donne's Meditation 17 says that the death of any man diminishes me. However, Robert Jordan maintains his individuality. In fighting for the cause of the Spanish people, Robert Jordan is a part of the cause, but at the same time he has "his individuality which shines out bright and clear among other people."

The title suggests that death is inevitable. However, the importance of a man lies in making the best use of his life before he meets his death. The real worth of man's life does not lie in accumulating wealth for oneself alone, but in giving up his like for cumulative good of the whole mankind. Robert Jordan dies for others. Therefore, *For Whom The Bell Tolls* is not a depressing book

The Plot

Robert Jordan was a young American teacher who was in Spain fighting with the Loyalist guerrillas. The Loyalists were to make an offensive movement after three days. Jordan's most important mission was to blow up the bridge which would be of great strategic importance during the Loyalist offensive movement Jordan was behind the Fascists line. He was instructed to make contacts with Pablo, the leader of a guerrilla band and with his wife, Pilar, who was really a strong figure among the partisans. The partisans was the Russian term "for guerrilla work behind the times." The strategy was to make an advance on La Granja if the bridge is blown up. Robert Jordan was entrusted with the job of blowing up the bridge. He was to seek co-operation from Pable and Pilar. Pilar was the wife of Pablo. Pablo, was weak and a drunken braggart. Pilar was strong and trustworthy. She was devoted to the cause of Loyalists Jordan knew that she would carry out her part of the mission without caring for danger to her life. Jordan was required to blow up the bridge after the attack has started.

> I will tell you. But you are to use the date and hour only as an indication of a probability. You must be ready for that time. You will blow the bridge after the attack has started. You see? He indicated with the pencil. 'That is the only road on which they can get up tanks, or artillery, or even move a truck towards the pass which I attack. I must know that bridge is gone. Not before, so it can be repaired if the attack is postponed. No it must go when the attack starts and I must know it is gone.

Jordan studied the bridge from all angles. He made final plans to blow up the bridge at the proper moment. Jordan had blown up many bridges and three trains. This particular operation was a little difficult because everything was to be done on a split second schedule. However, the communist leadership in the war was disorganized. The Loyalists were out-numbered, moreover, the plans of offensive were frequently changed, which made the work of blowing up the bridge more complicated. However, Robert Jordan had said "I will do it all right." Jordan went to the cave hide-out of Pablo and Pilar. He met a beautiful young girl Maria. She had escaped from the Fascists. She has been starved and tortured and raped. She felt unclean. Jordan also met Anselmo. He was a loyal old man who would follow orders at the risk of his life. Anselmo hated to kill people, However, Arselmo would kill if he were given such orders.

Jordan loved the desperate guerillas. They could cruel. The guerrillas were cruel towards the fascists. Their poverty made them cruel against the Fascists it seemed from poverty and ignorance. Jordan also hated the Fascists because they came from the wealthy an ambitious people of Spain. Maria's story of her suffering at the hands of Fascists filled Jordan with such hatred that he could have killed a thousand of them, though like Anselmo he hated to kill Jordan fell deeply in love with Maria. She came hire sleeping bag at night. The love for Maria made him feel that he was not ready to die. He told Maria that one day they would be married. But there was lurking fear in his mind about the future.

Jordan made careful plans of blowing up the bridge. His work was almost ruined by Pablo's treachery. On the night before blowing up of the bridge, Pablo deserted after stealing and destroying the explosives and the detonators hidden in Jordan's pack Pablo returned in the morning. He was repentant but the damage had, already been done, Now Jordan would have to blow the bridge with hand grenade. It was a much more dangerous method. Jordan despised Pablo but he forgave him.

Jordan worked quickly and carefully. Each person had. a specific job to do. First Jordan and Anselmo had to kill sentries. Pablo and his guerrillas attacked the Fascists lines to prevent their crossing before the bridge was blown up at the beginning of the bombing attack over the Fascists lines. When Jordan heard the explosion of the bombs, the bridge was blown up. The operation was successful. Jordan was sage but Anselmo was killed. Jordan was sorry for Anselmo. He would not have been killed if Pablo had not stolen the detonators. Jordan wanted to kill Pablo. But his duty was otherwise. Jordan saw to the meeting place of the guerrilla where he met Pablo, Pilar, Maria and two remaining guerrillas. Pablo was herding the extra horses. He told Jordan that all the other guerrillas had been killed. Jordan knew that Pablo had ruthlessly killed them to get their horses. Pablo admitted his slaughter. He had no qualms of conscience because they did not belong to his band.

There was the problem to cross a road that led to safety. The road could be swept by Fascists gunfire. Jordan knew that the first-two people would have good. chance to cross the road before the Fascists became alert. Pablo knew the road to safety. Jordan put him on, the first horse. Maria was second. Jordan wanted to save her. Pilar was to go next, the two remaining guerrillas. Last of all Jordan crossed the road. The first-four people crossed safely. Jordan's horse fell on Jordan's legs because it was wounded by Fascist's bullet. The others dragged him across the road. He was safely taken out of the line of fire. But Jordan knew that he could not go on. He was so badly injured that he could not ride a horse. Pablo and Pilar understood that Jordan could not be taken away. Maria begged to stay with him. Jordan told Pilar to take Maria when he gave the signal. He told Maria that she must go on because as long as she lived, he lived also When the time came, she had to be put on her horse and taken away. Jordan could not be taken to the place of safety.

Jordan was sure to meet his death. He showed grace under pressure.

Jordan waited for the Fascists troops. He propped himself against the tree, holding his gun across his knees. As he waited he thought over the events that had brought him to that place. He was satisfied that what he had done was right. At the same time he knew that his side might not win for many years. Jordan also knew if the common people kept dying, some day they would win. He hoped that the people would be prepared when that day came. Moreover, they would. not like to kill and torture the people. On the other hand, they will struggle for peace and freedom. He felt at the end that his own part in the struggle had not been in vain:

> I have fought for what I believed in for a year. Now if we win here we will win everywhere. The world is a fine place and worth the fighting for and hate very much to leave it. And you had a lot of luck; he told himself to have had such a good life. (p.440)

Jordan saw that after all his mission was successful:

> He was completely integrated, now and he took a good long took at everything. Then he looked up at the sky. There were big white clouds in it. He touched the palm of his hand against the pine needles where he lay and he touched the bark of the pine trunk that he lay behind. (p. 444)

As he saw the first Fascist approaching, Robert Jordan smiled. He was ready. Symbolism and Irony

Hemingway's aim as a writer is to tell the truth which such a high standard of fidelity that it produces truer account than anything factual can be Ernest Hemingway says in *Death In the Afternoon.*

> ... .. and I found the greatest difficulty, aside from knowing truly that you really felt, rather than what

> you were supposed to feel, and had been Taught to feel, was to put down what really happened in action, what the actual things were which produced the emotions that you experienced.

Hemingway's style proved a tool of precision for laying bare the ambiguities of human life.

The Iceberg Principle

Hemingway has shown ruthless economy of words. He never uses a superfluous word. It makes Ernest Hemingway a highly implicative writer. Hemingway says in *Death In The Afternoon*: "The dignity of the movement of an iceberg is due to only one-eighth of its being above water." This dignity of iceberg has been obtained by the narrative technique of irony and symbolism. The title of the novel *For Whom The Bell Tolls* is highly suggestive. Ernest Hemingway leaves many things unsaid. He believes in the dictum: : "Less is more." Moreover, Ernest Hemingway is always straight and simple in his narrative pattern. The use of symbols enlightens the reader's mind with the seven-eighth part of the iceberg. T.S. Eliot attained the effect of poetic shorthand by the artistic use of myths and legends. Ernest Hemingway never uses myths or legends derived from scriptures. On the other hand, he uses symbols which are suggestive of the inner mind of the hero.

Artistic Use of Symbolism

Symbolism is comparison between the abstract and the concrete with one of the terms of comparison being merely suggested. The suggestiveness is the main characteristic of Hemingway. However, Hemingway, never uses symbols in a conscious way. He has used the symbols which awaken in the mind of the reader certain emotional responses through the laws of association. In an interview with Robert Manning, Hemingway said: "No good book has ever been written that has in it symbols arrived at before hand and stuck in." He took a piece of French bread and said, "That kind of symbol sticks out like raisins in raisin read. Raisin bread is all right, but plain bread is better." With the use of symbols, Hemingway has transformed the novel about the Spanish Civil War into a parable of the artistic nature. The tragedy of the bridge becomes the tragedy of the Spanish earth and its people.

The opening lines of the novel has the symbolic significance:

> He lay flat on the brown, pine-needle floor of the forest, his chin on his folded arms and high overhead. The wind blew in the tops of the Pine trees. The mountain side sloped gently where he lay but below it was steep and he could see the dark of the oiled road winding through the pass. There was a stream alongside the road and far down the pass he saw a mill beside the stream and the falling water of the dam, white in the summer sunlight.

The above lines are not merely descriptive but also suggestive of Robert Jordan's mental conditions. He lay flat. Lying flat is the symbol of impending doom. Robert Jordan is in a state of existential despair. The land is brown and not green. The brown land symbolizes the ravages of the Spanish Civil War. "The pine-needle flow," is highly symbolical of the thorny way of life under Fascist terrorism. Mountain is the symbol of immortality. Ernest Hemingway has taken pains to describe the position were Robert Jordan lay. Below it was steep. The steep slope is symbolical of the hard and rough life. Robert Jordan could see the dark of the oiled road. It is symbolical of the hard and difficult task of getting free from the Fascist tyranny. However, he sees the stream alongside the road. Stream is the symbol of life. The falling water of the dam is suggestive of constructive use of the national resources bringing fertility and prosperity to the common people. Therefore, the falling water of the dam is white in the summer sunlight.

By the end of the novel again we find Robert Jordan lying on the pine-needles. He takes long look at the road in the village:

> Robert Jordan saw there were on the slop, close to him now and below he saw the road and the bridge and the long lines of vehicles below it. He was completely integrated now and he took a good long look at everything. Then he looked up at the sky. There were big white could sin it. He touched the palm of his hand against the pine trunk that he lay behind. (p. 444)

The novel has taken the full circular motion. Robert Jordan touched the palm of his hand against pine needles where he lay. This is the symbol of his love for the mother earth. At the same time he looked up at the sky. Looking up at the sky is the symbol of his idealism to identify himself with the cause of humanity. There were big white coulds in the sky. The white clouds are the symbol of immortality gained through the sacrifice of his life for the good of others. In the beginning of the novel, Robert Jordan saw "the falling water of the dam, white in the summer sunlight." By the end of the novel, he saw big white cloud in the sky. Now Robert Jordan was completely integrated. The opening and the ending of the novel has symbolic significance. Ernest Hemingway has a peculiar liking for the long hair of the woman. The hair of the woman is the symbol of feminity. In the story *A Cat in the Rain*, The girl is tired of looking like a boy. She wants long hair to tie in a knot. Robert Jordan found in Maria the fulfillment of his wife. Maria was badly treated by the Fascists. Her head was regularly shaved. It is symbolical of her purity being ravished time and again. Yet her hair grew fast. It is the symbol of Maria's purity. It is the symbol of the fascist terrorism. She was not unclean. That is why Robert Jordan has spiritual affinity with her. Robert Jordan calls her "Rabbit" and "a colt." The use of these two words has symbolic significance. Ernest Hemingway was masculine writer. He has only heroes and practically no heroines. However, Maria and Pilar play an important role in the novel. They are not whores.

> The sleeping bag is the symbol of mother's womb. Jordan and Maria slept together in the sleeping bag which becomes the symbol of home where there is security, love and affection. Rain is the symbol of disaster. Ernest Hemingway has seen the misery of the refugees in the Graeco-Turkish War in the midst of rains. The rainy days depressed the spirits of Hemingway. In the novel *For Whom The Bell Tolls*, he impending doom is symbolized by the untimely snow-fall and grey and heavy clouds, "Robert Jordan looked up at the thick grey of the sky with the sun gone faintly yellow, and how as he watched gone completely and the grey becoming uniform so that it was soft and heavy; the grey now cutting off the tops of the mountains." (p.172)

Milk stands for the comforts of home life. The aeroplanes, symbolize the Fascist terrorism. Pillar gave Robert Jordan bowl of coffee. She handed him a can of condensed milk. Robert Jordan remarked:

> There milk? What luxury! There is every think, she said. And since the planes there is much fear where did you say there went? Robert Jordan dripped some of the thick milk into his coffee from the slit out in the can, wiped the can on the rism of the cup, and stirred the coffee until it was a light brown.'

Robert Jordan wiped the can on the rim of the cup. This act shows Robert Jordan's concern for the happy home life. Robert Jordan is busy in making the plans of blowing up the bridge. At heart he does not like this act of violence. However, this is the mystery and ambiguity in life. Jordan had been involved in bridge blowing twice. He had never liked the act of blowing up the bridge. However, he does it for the sake of the greater good of the mankind: "Twice I have been on the wheel and twice it has gone around and come back to where it started and I am taking no more rides on it." (p. 217)

Death is associated with 'Nada' but life is like a field of grain. It is like a hawk in the sky. Robert Jordan thinks about drying and living:

> Dying was nothing and he had no picture of it nor fear of it in his mind. But living was a hawk in the sky. Living was an earthen jar of water in the dust of the threashing with the grain failed out and the chaff blowing. Living was a horse between your legs and a carbine under one leg and a hill and valley and the hills beyond. (p. 296)

Ernest Hemingway has used different symbols to show the importance of living and how difficult it is to keep in living in these days.

The flask of water is the symbol of life. After being severely wounded after bowing up of the bridge, Robert Jordan finds his flask of water missing. This is the clear indication that he is going to lose his life.

Robert Jordan remembers the hotel called Gaylord's where the Russian directors of the Republican movement had congregated: "Gaylord's symbolized the cold practical, hard headed, cynical ruthlessness of the comintern mind, completely unsentimental and in no way deceived by the propaganda which daily originated and disseminated."

Use of Irony

The title of the novel *For Whom The Bell Tolls* is itself an index of its strongly ironic theme. The death knell does not toll for a particular man, but it tolls for everyone of us. Both, the rightist and leftist accused Hemingway of having gone over the other side. Robert Jordan feels that both the sides have come thing wrong in them. Of course, no man is an island. But the predicament of human life is of such a force that none of us can depend on better fortune than that of Jordan.

> His affiliation with the Loyalists is no simple partisan allegiance, and to extend and support the heroes explicit awareness of the inevitable contradictions of his position. Hemingway poses a series of situations pregnant with irony.

The sarcastic remark about the gipsies have hyper-ironic over-tones against the love of gypsies for the bear:

> 'Yes', Anselmo said, 'the gipsies believe the beat to be a brother of man.' 'so do the Indian in America.' Robert Jordan said, "And when they kill a bear they apologize. They put his skill in a tree and they ask him to forgive them before they leave it.' (p.42)

There is a stroke of irony when Anselmo says about the gypsies, "To them it is not a sin to kill outside the tribe. They deny this, but it is true." There is the undertone of sympathy beneath the ironic description of the movement.

They were walking now close together in the dark and he spoke softly, sometimes turning his head as he climbed. It would not kill even a Bishop. I could not kill a proprietor of any kind. I would make them work each day as we have worked in the fields and as we work in the mountains with the timber all of the rest of their lives. So they would see what man is born to. That they should sleep where we sleep. That they should eat as we eat. But above all that they should work. Thus they would learn. And they would survive to enslave thee again. To kill them teaches nothing. Anselmo said, you cannot exterminate them because then their seed comes more with greater hatred. Prison is nothing. Prison only makes hatred. That all enemies should learn. (p. 43)

Pilar's accounts of the start of the movement is full of irony:

> Outstanding is Pilar's account of the start of 'the movement' in Pablo's home town with its unflinching report of the steadily mounting sadism which infused the execution of the local Fascists. There is a remarkable tone to this report as if Pillar were at confession, anxious to tell the whole truth and omitting not even the most shameful details, yet seeking at the same time to make it understood how these grimly acts could have occurred among normally decent Spanish peasants. She tells how at first many of the peasants were sickened by Pablo's plan to flail the Fascists down between a double line of misleading to the edge of a steel cliff. But within the ironic frame of the entire episode, in relation to the book, there are lesser ironies for it is the cowardly behaviour of the Fascists themselves that brings these peasants to a pitch of mob hatred and violence equal to Pablo's inveterate cruelty.

The irony of Jordan' self-conscious ambivalence is heightened by juxtapositions in the modest of El Sordo's great last fight. We are suddenly given a decidedly sympathetic portrait of Lt. Berrendo, second in command of the Fascist cavalry. Carlos baker says:

> The novel *For Whom The Bell Tolls,* is Hemingway's fullest work so far in scope and artistic realization, and to its fulfillment the ambiguity of irony contributes an essential part.

Hemingway has used techniques of symbolism of technique and irony and has used them well.

3

Robert Jordan: The Hemingway Hero

The hero of *For Whom The Bell Tolls* is Robert Jordan. He is a young American teacher of Spanish. He has come to Spain to fight for the Loyalists in Civil War. He has come to Spain because he identifies himself with the Spanish people. Though an American, he has genuine concern for the suffering mankind. Robert Jordan is "no island." The sufferings of the people "diminish" him.

Hemingway made use of his firsthand experience in his novel. Many of his friends appear in the novel, sometimes under their actual names an sometimes in this disguises of fictional names. Robert Jordan owes something to the courageous figure of Major Robert Merriman of the Fifteenth International brigade.

A Wounded Hero

Robert Jordan's idealism has been dampened where he comes in contact with the harsh realities of Spanish struggle. He has the experience of blowing up the bridges but this time he feels hesitation and nervousness. This feeling is the result of existential despair:

> He would not think about that. That was not this business. That was Golz's business. He has only one thing to do and that was what he should think about and he must think if clearly and take everything as

> it came along and not worry. To worry wȧs as bad as to afraid. It simply made things more difficult.

However, Robert Jordan does not suffer from self-pity. He does not parade his troubles before others to win their sympathies. He has a mission to fulfill, and he does at the cost of his life. Robert finds death and violence all around but he never gives up his efforts. By the end of the novel, he is seriously wounded but he does not commit suicide as his father has done. He gets courage from the example of his grandfather who has fought bravely in American war of independence. Robert Jordan shows grace under pressure because of his moral courage. Ernest Hemingway drew heavily from his personal life in giving the character of Robert Jordan. Jordan is the semi-autobiographical hero. There is much similarity between Jordan and Ernest Hemingway. Jordan's parents are clearly modeled on Dr. and Mrs. Hemingway Jordan's father had shot himself to death like Dr. Edmonds Hemingway. Ernest called his father a coward and his mother a bitch. Robert Jordan also says about his father.

> I'll never forget how sick it made me the first time. I knew he was acarbarde. Go on, say it in English coward. Its easier when you have it said and there is never any point in referring to a son of a bitch by some foreign term. (p.320)

However, Robert Jordan consoles himself "Better not think at all." Robert Jordan does not want to be a mere soldier: "Well, I don't to be soldier," From the beginning of the novel, Robert Jordan has the premonition if impending doom. He does not fee elated as a conventional here does while engaged in destructive activities.

Hemingway, was badly mounded in a mortar shell. Describing this experience he said, "I felt my soul or something coming right out of my body like you'd pull handkerchief out of a pocket of one corner. It flew around and then came back and went in again and I was not dead any more." The would had crippled not only his body but his mind as well. Like Hemingway his heroes too sustain incurable wounds. They are physically wounded people. Nick Adams is wounded in the spine. Jake Barnes (The Sun Also Rises), is impotent as the result of the wound. Fredrick Henry (A Farewell to Arms), and Harry (The Snows of Kilimanjaro) have wounded legs and Robert Jordan (For Whom The Bell Tolls) is mortally wounded. Even the old man Santiago, feels something breaking, inside him when he fights with that big martin.

Gradual Change from Despair to Hope and Faith

Since his arrival in Spain, Robert Jordan has come face to face with the cynicism of these in power. Most of the common people for whom he is fighting are no longer interested in the war. They are also not willing to die for the cause. Robert Jordan has become aware of the realities. He is not a communist, but simply an anti-fascist. However, during the four-day time span of novel, Robert Jordan is a man in transition. It the beginning the is attracted by ideas of courage and humanity. He slowly moves from the waning belief of the cause to a new appreciation of the importance of the individual man. In the closing pages of the novel, Jordan has done his duty for the Spanish cause. He thinks of committing suicide but does not do so. He changes his mind. He wants to stay alive so that he can be of service to him. The change from gloomy despair to sunny hope and faith comes to him through his love for Maria. In the end he feels that life is worth living. His love for maria gives him an integrated personality:

> Maria is my rue love and my brother and I never had a true love, I never had a wife. She is my sister and I never has a sister and my daughter and I never will have a daughter. I hate to leave a thing that is so good. (p.360)

In the beginning of the novel, Robert Jordan has called

his father a coward, but later on, in the novel, he has nostalgic remembrances of his father's farewell to him at the platform:

> Robert Jordan has not felt this young since he had taken the train at Red Lodge to go down to Billing to get the train there to go away to school for the first time. He had been afraid to go and he did not want anyone to know it... But his moustache had been moist and his eyes were dampt with emotion and Robert Jordan had been so embarrassed by all of it, the damp religious sound of the prayer, and by his father kissing him good-bye, that he had felt suddenly so much older than his father and sorry for him that he could hardly bear it. (p.381)

Robert Jordan is a man of courage. He carries his plans carefully for the greater good of humanity:

I have fought for what I believed in for a year now. If we win here we will win everywhere. The world is a fine place and worth the fighting for and I have very much to leave it. And you had a lot of luck, he told himself. (p.440)

Robert Jordan shows grace under pressure. He has three days and three nights and he is thankful for them: "Dying a only bad when it takes a long-time and hurts so much that it humiliates you. That is where you have all the luck, see? You don't have any of that." (p. 441)

Not a Code Hero

Ernest Hemingway has portrayed the character of Robert Jordan in an artistic way. He carefully plans the blowing up the bridge. Each and every detail is threshed out. He even tolerates the selfishness of Pablo. But he never stoops low to achieve his aim. He takes up the blowing up of the bridge with a missionary zeal. There is definite moral growth in him. On the personal level, he hated Pablo. He hated the inefficiency of the Loyalitst Commanders in changing the plans of attack. Yet, he never budges an inch from his duty. Hemingway's code heroes like Wilson stop shortage a certain stage. They do the duty for the sake of duty. But Robert Jordan does his duty for the sake of fulfilling mission taken upon himself for the zeal of service to humanity. Robert attains the mystical heights when he bids goodbye to Maria: "There is o good-bye, Guapa, because we are not apart." (p.437) Robert Jordan shows concern for the safety of Maria. He says: "Do not turn around. Pat thy foot in, yes, thy foot in help her up, he said to Pilar." (p. 437)

Robert Jordan has the satisfaction of doing the best of his capacity However, he has the spirit of self-sacrifice. He may not do anything for himself, but he can do for others:

> Each one does what he can. You can do nothing for yourself but perhaps you can do something for another. (p.439)

Robert Jordan knows well that his act of blowing up the bridge does not mean much, he has faith in the future of mankind: "If this attack is not good, another one will be." (p.442)

Robert Jordan is the Hemingway hero who stands by his ideals. He is the prototype of Hemingway. The Nobel Prize citation praised *For Whom The Bell Tools* in which an American Champaign of liberty fights man's dignity, a book in which the writer's personal feelings seem more deeply involved than anywhere else.

Of all heroes, Robert Jordan comes closest to Ernest Hemingway. Like Hemingway, Robert Jordan has written a book on Spain and the Spanish people (p.230) Like Hemingway, Jordan is an artist who is fully aware of the threat of Fascist domination. Robert Jordan shows fully well Hemingway, the man and the artist.

4

Personages

Hemingway is the keen observer of the human nature. He prefers concrete things to abstract things. Being a keen observer of human nature, Hemingway goes deep in the study of human nature through his characters. The principle of characterization-in-depth is very strong in *For Whom The Bell Tolls*.

Character of Maria

Maria is the heroine of the novel *For Whom The Bell Tolls*. Hemingway took the name Maria from a nurse whom he met at Mataro:

> Maria, the heroine, bore the name of the nurse whom Ernest had met at Mataro in the spring in 1938, although her physical characteristic including her blonde hair. 'Like a wheatfield in the wing' were evidently designed as a secret tribute to Martin Gellhorn.

Hemingway was a masculine writer. In his novels, the female characters did not play a dominant role. But in this novel, Maria played a definite role by creating good influence on the hero Robert Jordan. Through her character, Ernest Hemingway has shown the atrocities of the Fascists.

Murder of Maria's Parents

Maria was the victim of Fascist tyranny. Her father was the mayor of the village and an honorable man. Her mother was a good catholic. They shot Maria's mother because of her husband's politics. Maria's father was Republican. Her father said "Long live Republic," because being shot dead. Maria's mother was also killed She said, "Long live my husband who is the Mayor of his village." (p.33). Maria and other girls of the village were not killed. They were paraded through the streets:

> We were tied by the wrists in a long line of girls and women and they herded us up by the hill and through the streets to the square. (p. 332)

Maria narrated all the brutal acts of the Fascists. Robert Jordan could not hear the whole account. He said. "Do not take more about it. "Do not tell me any more for I cannot bear any hatred now." (p. 334)

Her Faminine Qualities

Maria had the moral courage to narrate all the ugly incidents. She had the sense of self-respect. She wanted to clear her position. She said to Robert Jordan:

> Never did I submit to anyone. Always I fought and always it too two of them or more to do me the harm. One would sit on my head and hold me. I tell thee for thy pride. (p. 331)

She did not want to keep Robert Jordan in dark about the ugly things done to her. The incidents were too heavy for her. She got emotional relief by narrating those incidents to Robert Jordan:

> But that it were better never to speak of it unless it came on me as a black thing as it had been before and then that telling it to thee might rid me of it. (p.331)

After meeting Robert Jordan, she felt at ease. Yet she could not forget the brutal way in which his father and mother were slaughtered: "There is the sorrow for my parents, always. But that there will be always."

Her Role in Blowing up the Bridge

Maria was with Robert Jordan in the operation of blowing up the bridge. She took active interest for the sake of Robert Jordan. Moreover, she also wanted to help the cause of the Republic. It was her faithfulness that she wanted to stay with Robert Jordan. "Nay, I stay with thee," said Maria. Robert Jordan had real concern for her safety. The first man to cross the road was Pablo because he knew the road. The second has all the chances of crossing the road. So Robert Jordan, despite his serious condition, made arrangements to send Maria safety:

> 'Thou,' he said to Maria, 'go second as they cross the road. First is not so bad though it seems bad. Second is good. It is later that they are always watching for.' (p. 431)

When Maria insisted on staying, Jordan said, "You must not be selfish rabbit, you must do your duty now."

Edmust Wilson levels a charge against Hemingway's heroines that they are "amoeba-like". But it is not true in the case of Maria. Robert Jordan wanted Maria to do her duty. So he wanted to send her to the place of safety, "Thou will go now for us both," said Robert Jordan.

Symbol of Home

Robert Jordan had real love for Maria, because she was pure at heart. Robert Jordan said, "I care for her very much."

Maria recovered from the shock of at rock of atrocities through the love of Robert Jordan. Jordan had also transition from hatred to sunny hope and faith through his contact with Maria. Maria stands for the normal in the midst of a terrible abnormality:

> The significance of Maria... is finally symbolic. In the lonely alien region of the Guardarramas, she comes to stand as the image of 'home.'

Maria is the victim of the cruelty and violence. She is so much deprived of the finer elements of nature that good experiences arouse a sense of disbelief in her. Through her character, Ernest tries to arouse our sympathy for those women whose past is scared and future insecure. Maria is a constructive force in the midst of destructive ones. She is the embodiment of love and humility. Maria is a completing agent for the hero Robert Jordan. In turn, she is completed by her association with him. Maria represents normal domesticity vanquished by war.

Character of Pablo

Pable is a fictional character. Ernest Hemingway drew heavily own his experiences as in drawing his characters. In the character of Pablo, Ernest Hemingway has shown the attitude of the common people towards the cause of the Spanish Civil War. Pablo was the leader of the land of guerrillas who were supposed to help Robert Jordan in blowing up the bridge.

Pablo's Unco-operative Attitude

Pablo's was sullen and unco-operative. He did not want to take part in Jordan's assignment. He did not want that his people should take part in blowing up the bridge because it involved danger to his people. He was more interested in blowing up the train because it involved loot while in blowing up the bridge there was no such gain. Robert Jordan flattered Pablo. But Pablo was realistic enough not to be flattered by Robert Jordan. He remained morose and unco-operative.

Pablo's Beard-Stubbled Face

Ernest Hemingway has given the details of Pablo's physique to give us an idea about him:

> It was almost round and his head was round and set close to his shoulders. His eyes were small and set too wide apart and his ears were small and set close to

> his head. He was a heavy man about five feet ten inches tall and his feet and hands were large. His nose had been broken and his mouth was cut at one corner and the line of the scar across the upper lip and lower jaw showed through the growth of beard over his face. (p. 13)

Pablo refused to help Jordan with the sacks. Anselmo scolded Pablo for being a brute and a beast:

> Art thou a brute? Yes, Art thou a beast? Yes, many times. Hast thou a brain? Nay. None. Now we come for something of consummate importance and thee, with they dwelling place to be undisturbed, puts thy fox-hope before the interests of humanity. (p. 15)

Pablo's Talent

> Robert Jordan had to tolerate Pablo because he had the necessary talent to do the job of blowing up the bridge. Agustin said, "But the talent is Pablo." Pilar was correct in her remark to Pablo: "From one year of war thou hast become lazy, a drunkard and a coward." (p. 56)

A Murderous Bastard

Pablo took part in blowing up the bridge. He provided necessary material. He had stolen the detonators and explosives. So it was necessary to use hand grenade which took the life of Anselmo. Immediately after blowing up the bridge, Pablo killed other members simply to obtain their horses. " We have plenty of horse now, Ingles,' Pablo panted. "Good' Robert Jordan said , 'The murderous bastard,' he thought." (p. 428) Pablo had no remorse. He simply said that they were not of his tribe. Pablo said, "this is war. One cannot do what one would wish." (p. 429)

Sick of War

Pablo was sick of war. He was unwilling to die for the

cause of the Loyalists. At first he deserted the guerillas but later on, came back to take part in blowing up the bridge. Here we get parallelism in the actions of Pablo and Jordan:

Pablo deserts, an action which is thematically parallel to Jordan's later contemplation of suicide. But, again paralleling Jordan's action, he returns because he is only one who can lead the group to safety after the battle.

Though he came back but he felt that there was loneliness that could not be borne.

Similarity with Jordan

At first glance it appears that the characters of Pablo and Jordan are dissimilar. Pablo is morose and unco-operative. Jordan is full of missionary zeal. As the novel progresses, we find that Pablo and Jordan are basically alike.

Both are experiencing the same transition, but with a difference "that Pablo has progressed further along the scale than has Jordan" Pablo had accepted the realities of the war to which Jordan had been trying to adapt himself.

There is change in Pablo. He feels sorry for Jordan. He knows the hopelessness of the situation. He asks Jordan to talk to Maria. Jordan asks Pablo to think of the Republic.

> 'I think you would do better in the Republic,'
> Robert Jordan said.
> 'Nay, I am for Credos.'
> 'Use they head,'
> 'Talk to her now,' Pablo said.
>
> 'There is little time, I am sorry thous hast this, ingles,'
>
> Since I have it—Robert Jordan said, 'Let us not speak of it. But use thy head. Thou hast much head, Use it,'
> 'Why would I not?' said Pablo... (p. 435)

Pablo's remarks "Why would I not?" suggests that Pablo is experiencing a change in himself.

Pablo played an important role in the novel. According to Carlos Baker, we can "recognize in Pablo the rude outlines of a debased and sulking Ajax/."

Pablo is a 'specific Judas,' as his stealing of the detonators shows. He is a symbol for the "general canker of defeatism, gnawing the tissues of republican morale from within, and leading to the large betrayal."

Pablo's role adds suspense to the novel. Hemingway has devoted many chapters to describe Pablo's murderous acts. This is done not to pile horror upon horror. Pablo has neither moral nor morale. Pablo's character also shows the callous attitude of the people towards the higher values of life. Through Pablo, Hemingway tries to show the dehumanizing effect of war on human beings.

Character of Pilar

Pilar Played an important role in the novel. Ernest Hemingway derived the name from the blessed Virgin of Pilar:

> She is the patron of all-Spain, and the cathedral and the cathedral del Pilar – one of the two cathedrals in Saragossa – is dedicated to her. The cathedral is in Commemoration of the Virgin Mary on a Pilar on January 2, A.D. 40.

Ernest also named his cruiser as The Pilar. Pauline also chose as one of her secret nicknames when she first fell in love with Ernest. Through the character of Pilar, Ernest Hemingway gave to the reader the background information of the 'movement' of Spain. She narrated the beginning of the 'movement' She gave the graphic description of the way of life before the war. She gave us the information about the courage of Pablo before he ruined himself. Moreover, she read Jordan's palm and prepared the feeling of impending doom.

Mujer of Pablo

Pilar was the *mujer* of Pablo. She was with Pablo for several years. Before it she was with a few matadors. Pilar was brave and barbarous. The gipsy said about Pilar:

> Something very barbarous. If you think Pablo is ugly you should see his woman. But brave. A hundred times braver than Pablo. But something barbarous. (p.28)

She spoke obscene language. Being a gipsy woman she had no sophisticated manners. But at heart she was kind and sympathetic. She was kind towards Maria. She kept Maria under her protection. Agustin told Jordan, "You cannot imagine with what fierceness she guarded her." (p.276). Pilar read Jodan's palms. She could understand that Jordan was not going to live long. She refused to divulge what she had seen. Moreover, she allowed Maria and Jordan to meet together. Jordan's love had a healthy effect on the mind of Maria. Jordan also experienced a change in him. Thus Pilar was responsible for bringing transition in Jordan.

Pilar was realistic enough to tell Jordan about herself:

> Vamos, I'm not ugly. I was born ugly. All my life I have been ugly. You, Ingles, who know nothing about women. Do you know what it is to be ugly all your life and inside to feel that you are beautiful? (p.95)

Pilar thought philosophically, "Life is very curious... I would have made a good man, but I am all woman and all ugly." (p.95). Pilar's account of her ugly life brought a change in Jordan and he told her that he was not ugly. Pilar laughed and said, "Has it begun to work with three?"

Pilar was forty-eight years old. Like any other woman she had psychological problems. "At time many things tire me," said Pilar angrily.

Her Qualities of Leadership

Pablo was not interested in co-operating with Jordan in blowing up the bridge. Pilar was in favour of supporting Jordan. Ultimately, Pablo abdicated the leadership Pilar became the leader. The gypsies owed allegiance to her. They extended co-operation to Jordan, simple because Pilar was with him.

> 'To me the bridge means nothing.'
> One of the brothers said, 'I am for the mujer of Pablo.
> 'Equally,' said the other brother.
> 'Equally,' the gipay said. (p 54)

> Pilar possessed the qualities of mind and heart to become the leader of the guerillas. As a good leader she know the right order of priorities. The first task was to blow up the bridge. "Afterward we will have time for other projects." (p.54). While helping in blowing up the bridge, Pilar said, "It is speed that counts." (p.418)

Change in Pilar

After the blowing up the bridge, Pilar went to Jordan. Pilar slit his trouser with her knife to see the wound. On seeing snapped-off thigh bone of Jordan. Pilar's face had the "same expression as Maria's." Jordan realized the intensity of her feelings. He told Pilar to go and not to say there:

> She went away with head down without saying anything nor looking back and Robert Jordan could see her shoulders shaking. (p.436)

Jordan had faith ion Pilar that she would take care of Maria as well as anyone could.

In the final pages of the novel, Pilar reached that stage of her transition in which she began to doubt the value of the Spanish cause. S.J.L. Galbraith says, "In the book we see Robert Jordan in transition from one concept to another.

Pablo, too, is on that same road, a few miles, as it was ahead of Jordan. And now we find Pilar traveling the same road, but "bringing up the rear."

Jordan shows a kind of spiritual relationship to Pilar. He can be, by turns, both tended and tough-minded. Pilar is arrogant to Pablo. She is considerate to Maria and Jordan. Pilar is associated with the mother image. She is patronizing and dominant. She is equipped with experience and knowledge. Above all, she is forgiving.

Charater of Anselmo

Anselmo appeared in the first chapter of the novel. Ernest Hemingway has not shown Anselmo's physical appearance as he has shown Pablo's physical appearance. Trough Anselmo's character, Ernest Hemingway has introduced mysticism in the novel. Robert Jordan forgot Anselmo's name. He regarded it as a bad segn.

Anselmo's Loyalty to Jordan

Anselmo was sixty-eight years old. Anselmo was inspired by the ideals of service to humanity. He scolded Pablo for his petty aims:

> 'That is unjust, "Said Pablo. ' expose the horses all the time for the cause,"
>
> 'Very little,' sais Anselmo scornfully.
>
> 'Very little in my judgement.'
>
> 'To steal, yes. To eat well, as. To murder, yes. To fight, no.' (p.19)

Pablo was a blood-thirsty murderer. Agustin was a fanatical hater. But Anselmo willingly edured discomfort out of loyalty to Jordan's trust. Unlike Pablo, Anselmo with the wisdom of years hated killing even when he admitted that it was necessary. Anselmo was not afraid of drying for a noble cause.

Sin of Killing

Ernest Hemingway has devoted in describing Anselmo's view on the sin of killing human beings:

> I hope, I am not for killing, Anselmo was thinking. I think that after the war there will have to be some great penance done for the killing. (p. 190)

Anselmo was of the opinion that those who like killing the people have always a "rollenness." He hoped that there would be certain days for penance. Anselmo felt the pangs of conscience on killing people. He had killed people earlier, and would do it, for a noble cause to end tyranny. But Anselmo was not of the "race of Pablo." Anselmo hated Fascists but did not like killing them, because, after all, they were human beings. Anselmo thought:

> To me it is a sin to kill a man. Even Fascists whom we must kill... No, I am against all killing. (p. 42)

When Robert Jordan killed the sentry, there were tears running down Anselmo's cheeks through grey beard, stubble. Ansolme did not mind killing an animal but he had quite different feelings in killing a man.

> In all hunting I have had an elation and no feeling of wrong. But to shoot a man gives a feeling as though one has struck one's own brother when you are grown men. (p. 416)

Of all the native Spaniards, none better exemplified the "right human norm" than Anselmo.

A Yardstick of Human Values

Anselmo's faith in God was shaken on seeing the atrocities. However, he hoped to be forgiven for his sing of killing human beings, but he did not know who would forgive him. He hoped that he would live in such a way, doing no harm to anyone that he would be forgiven. He could not understand why there could be so much killing if there was God. "If there were God, never would He have permitted what I have seen with my eyes." (p.43) Carlos Baker says:

> Anselmo's important function is to serve as a yardstick of human values, as Kent does in King Lear. That we should win the war the war and shoot nobody he cries fiercely. That we should govern justly and that all should participate in the benefits according as they have striven for them. And those who fought agaist us should be educated to see their error. The Republic must win and Ansemo will fight for the Republic. Yet much that he must do cuts clearly across the absolute Christian grain of this admirable old man. With Anselmo as a name, the tragedy of spain shows all the darker.

Anselmo was killed in blowing up the bridge. "Robert Jordan not to his feet... knelt by him." (p. 419). Anselmo met the death of a martyr. On his death we feel that war is a bad thing.

Anselmo possesses the qualities of mind and heart which are clearly associated with the character and personality of a martyr. Anselmo has gallantry. He has the staying power which helps him in his determination to last to the end of whatever is to come. He has ability to ignore pain. He has humility, piety and compassion. Anselmo is one of those nameless thousands who are the servants of good in the true sense of the word.

5

Thematic Study

The Place of *For Whom The Bell Tolls* in Literature

For Whom The Bell Tolls is most successful novel of Ernest Hemingway. It was published on October 21, 1940, and about nine weeks after publication about 189,000 copies were sold. By April, 4, 1941, sales had risen to 491,000 copies. Besides it, 565,000 copies were in print.[1] The Novel Prize Citation regarded it as a significant novel.[2] Carlos Baker regarded it as Ernest's best novel, and Malcom Coasley agreed with his opinion.[3]

For Whom The Bell Tolls is not a historical novel, or a propaganda novel. The Spanish Civil War was over. Hence there was no need of propaganda. With his eagle eyes Ernest Hemingway studies the Spanish Civil War. He had visited Spain so often that Spain was a part of him. It was not "one-visit" book.[4] He turned the incidents of the Spanish Civil War into a work of art. Ernest Hemingway, in his acceptance speech, said that a writer has an enduring appeal if we possessed 'degree of alchemy." *For Whom The Bell Tolls* has an enduring appeal. Prior to the acceptance, H.S. Nyberg, member of the Swedish Academy, made the following comment:

> The human problems which he Ernest Hemingway has treated are relevant to allo or us.... And few authors have exercised such a wide influence on contemporary literature in all countries.[5]

Carlos Baker regarded *For Whom The Bell Tolls* as Hemingway's King Lear.[6]

A Gensture of Sympathy for Anti-Fascist Movement

Ernest Hemingway hated Fascism. His hatred for Fascism began from the murder of Giacomo Nattcoti in June, 1924. Ernest was anti-Mussoline whom he regarded as a great bully. After his visit to Spain, Ernest delivered a passionate speech denouncing Fascism. He believed that Fascism is a lie told by bullies. So a writer who would not lie could not live or work under Fascism.

The novel *For Whom The Bell Tolls* showed Ernest's hatred for Fascism. Maria was made ugly by Fascists. Her parents were brutally murdered by the Fascists. Ernest described in details the atrocities committed on Maria by the Fascists to convince us how cruel and barbarous the Fascists were:

> And he struck me again and again across the face with the braids which had been nine and then he put the two of them in my mouth and tied them tight round my neck, knotting them in the back to make me gag and the two holding one laughed. (p. 333)
>
> On hearing the story of Maria, Robert Jordan was full of hatred as any man could be. He said, "Do not talk more about it. Do not tell me any more for I cannot bear hatred anymore." (p. 334).

By showing Robert Jordan's reactions, Ernest Hemingway tried to arouse people's sympathy for anti-Fascist movement.

A symbolic expression of Hemingway's Love for Spain

For Whom The Bell Tolls is the symbolic expression of the author's love for Spain. He wrote *Death in the Afternoon*, a book on bull-fighting. *Fifty Column* is another book of Hemingway on the *Spanish Civil War*. He helped Joris Ivens in making *The Spanish Earth*, a documentary film on the *Spanish War*. *The Fifty Column* was sympathetic to the Republic but did not clearly plead for the cause of the Loyalists. *In For Whom The Bell Tolls*, Hemingway maintained the balance and kept it from being on instrument of propaganda for either side in the civil war. Carlos Baker said, "For Whom the Bell Tolls" is not a study in black and white. It is a study of he betrayal of the Spanish people—both by what had been thrust upon them – and it is presented with that combination of sympathetic involvement and hard headed detachment which is the mark of the genuine artist... Its partisanship is the love of humanity.[7]

Robert Jordan who spoke for Hemingway, fought in the war because he loved Spain. Jordan believed in liberty, equality and fraternity. He had a feeling of consecration to a duty towards all the oppressed of the world. Hemingway had also similar feelings towards Spain. *For Whom The Bell Tolls* shows Hemingway's love for Spain.

Fulfilment of the Protagonist's Promises

Rober Jordan carefully planned the strategy of blowing up the bridge. Like Hemingway, he believed in doing things clearly. It was his self-imposed duty and he did it, not for money or fame, but for the oppressed people of Spain. Robert Jordan felt "This is a place here under the bridge. A home far away from home." (p. 411). Robert Jordan gave instructions not to indulge in useless killing. It was his anxiety to do the job in a clean way. Pillar once rebuked him saying, "Desist from thy lecture." (p. 422). Robert Jordan wanted that his mission should not end with the blowing up of the bridge. He made requests to Pablo to use his head and carry on the incomplete work. Robert Jordan fulfills his promises by rousing people's sympathy for the cause of the oppressed people. The Novel Prize citation says that Hemingway "prefers to leave the work of psychological reflection to his render."[8]

Hemingway's Style

Hemingway was awarded Novel Prize in 1954 for his powerful mastery of the art of the story-telling, and for his influence on the contemporary style. Hemingway evolved his style in the hard school of journalistic reporting:

> In the editorial office of the Kansas City newspaper where he served his apprenticeship, there was a kind of pressman's catechism, the first dictum of which was 'use short sentences, use short paragraphs.' Hemingway's purely technical training clearly led to an artistic self-discipline of uncommon strength. Rhetoric, he has said, is merely the blue sparks from the dynamo. His master in older American literature was Mark Twain in *Huckleberry Finn,* with its rhythmical stream of direct and unconventional narrative prose.[9]

For *Whom The Bell Tolls* has been conceived with care and executed with utmost brilliance:

> The great concentration with Hemingway achieves is partly dependent on his skill in keeping attention focused on the bridge while projecting the reader imaginatively far beyond that center of operations.[10]

The problem of blowing up the bridge is small in scale, but it is projected in such a way as to suggest a struggle of epical dimension:

> Indeed the novel *For Whom The Bell Tolls* is a living example of how, in modern times the epic must probably be projected.[11]

However, it is a tragic epic. It is a study in doom. Three is a mystical number. The Fascist plane are associated with the supernatural:

> The three passed and then came nine more, flying much higher in the minute pointed formations of threes, threes and threes. (p.74)

The novel touches the edge of the supernatural by the use of premonition. Pilar sees the coming of death in the lines of Jordan's hands. The Novel Prize citation calls Hemingway "one of the great authors of our time, one of those who, honestly and undauntedly, reproduces genuine features in the hard countenance of the age."

Nuance of Spoken Words

The Novel Prize citation calls Hemingway one of the great moulders of style. He produces "all the nuances of the spoken word with masterly skill." Robert Jordan is wounded. He cannot move. Maria wants to sty with him. She begins to cry:

> No, Guapa, don't, he said Listen. We will not go to Madrid now but I always go with thee, wherever thou goest. Understood? Listen to this wall, rabbit, he said. He knew there was sweating very much, but this has to be said and understood. Thou will go now, rabbit. But I go with thee. As long as there is one of us, there is both of us. Do you understand? (p. 436)

In the above passage, the heightened tone is conveyed in a simple language. Hemingway has used the Spanish word 'Guapa' in a forceful way. He has used the words 'understand.' Listen' repeatedly. Here Hemingway has reproduced the fine meanings of the spoken words. In the following sentences from *For Whom The Bell Tolls*, we find the truth of the remark that he products the nuances of spoken word:

> Now I thank fee for it. Now you are gong well and fast and far and we both go in thee. Now put thy hand here. Now put thy head down. Nay, put it down. That is right. Now I put my hand there. Good. Thou art so good. Now do not think more. Now thou art obeying. Not me but as both. The me in thee. Now you go for us both. Truly, we both go in three now. This I have

> promised thee. Thou art very good to go and very kind. (p. 437)

Nine sentences begin with 'Now' He has used the word 'go'. Several times. All the sentences are compact and compressed. The indemnity of emotion is conveyed in a simple and powerful language which touches poetical heights. In the following passage, there is the repetition of the word 'Now' with the remark 'now is thy prophet."

> This, that thy were not to have, they were having. They were having now and before and always and now and now and now. Oh, now, now, now, only now, and above all now, and there is no other now but thou now, and now is thy prophet. Now and for ever now. Come now, now, for there is no now but now. (p. 358)

Moments of Passivity

Hemingway's bare style of writing is very effective in taking note of the moments of passivity. He make an artistic use of physical and mental inactivity. By inactivity, it is not implied that all activity comes to an end. "What is suggested is a cessation of the action or movement controlled by human will and requiring the individuals conscious participation in it." In is the moment of vacuum.[12] When nothing is happening Hemingway recaptures the moment of passivity:

> Go on, come on. Go on. The roar was much that he could not hear what he was thinking. (p. 404)

In the above sentence Hemingway has captured the moment when the thought stands still and nervous mechanism in thrown out of gear. There is apparent contradiction, we can hear a speech. We cannot hear what we think. In the above sentence Hemingway has captured the movement when the "thought stands still and the nervous mechanism is throughout of gear."

Rhythmic Movement

Hemingway is a highly implicative writer. He makes an artistic use of repetition in such away that it produces third or fourth dimension in prose. He produces not only clarity and freshness but also rhythmic effect by the repetition of words:

> ... one and one is one, is one, is one, is one, is still one, is one descending, is one softly, is one longingly, is one kindly, is one happily, is one in goodness, is one to cherish. (p. 358)

Hemingway's word-pictures and images, combined with dialogues produce dramatic effect. According to Fenimore, there is Elizabethen tone in *For Whom The Bell Tolls*. In the Elizabethen age, the English possessed an epic language. Hemingway carefully tempars the language in his novel:

> Purely colloquial modern English and an English which belongs in its essence to the King James version of the Bible are brought together to mutual advantages.[13]

> The following sentence from the novel conveys the gist of Dorne's *Forbidding Mourning*. "There is no good-bye, Guapa, because we are not apart." (p. 437)

Vivid Dialogues

Hemingway's dialogues are chiseled. There is economy of words and the effect is much. The following conversation between Sordo and Jordan shows the power in the brevity of dialogues:

'Where?'

'Up the hill.'

'What kind?'

'Don't know name. With pans.'

'How many rounds?'

'Five pans.' (p. 141)

Kashkin, another dynamiter is shot death to relieve him of the agency of pain. Pilar does not know Kashkin's fate. She wants to confirm the facts:

> Was the one with the bad nerves and the strange name from there? Asked Pilar.
>
> 'Yes.'
>
> 'Where is he now?'
>
> 'Dead, as I told you.'
>
> 'You are from there, too?'
>
> 'Yes.'
>
> 'You see what I mean?' Pilar said to him. (p. 144)

The last line "You see what I mean?" is highly implicative. Pilar wants to say that Jordan's fate will be similar to that for Kashkin. Jordan feels nervousness on hearing the government of troops.

> 'Much troop movement.'
>
> 'Where?'
>
> 'Segovia, planes you saw?'
>
> 'Yes.'
>
> 'Bad, eh.'
>
> 'Bad.'
>
> 'Troop movement?' (p. 139)

Hemingway conveys the intensity of emotions through one or two words in a dialogue.

> 'Thou, thou art not worried anything?'
>
> 'No.'
>
> 'Truly?'
>
> 'No, not now.' (p. 359)

Use of Spanish Words and Phrases

Hemingway uses Spanish words and phrases effectively. The charm of his style lies in the fact that he is never obscure. On the other hand, the Spanish, words help us to understand the true character of the Spanish people.. The use of Spanish words gives local colour to the novel. Hemingway gives the Spanish words and phrases, and gives their meaning in English. This rendering is never given within brackets. This gives a peculiar charm and flow to his style.

The Spanish word 'Guapa' is quite often used. It means beautiful woman. The word 'anda' mans to go. The rendering of Spanish words in English has the added force of repetition. 'Anda', he said to hear, 'Go.' The word 'Nada' is a Spanish word meaning nothing. The concept of 'nada' is very clear in all-Hemingway's writings. Hemingway also uses words from other languages but he is always very accurate in his use of words. Moreover, the use of foreign words is not superfluous, or merely to show his learning and scholarship. Hemingway is always artistic. He is, no doubt, one of this epoch's great moulders of style.

Hemingway worked on this book for eighteen months. He did a good deal of reading for this novel. It contained no loose writing. Every word depended on every other word straight through the forty-three chapters. *For Whom The Bell Tolls* followed an architecture plan comparable to that of a Spanish butlring constructed in concentric circles arranged in such a way that from every point one could watch the action taking place at the centre. At first Hemingway thought of giving this noel the title *The Undiscovered Country*, but, later on, changed it to the present one. The present title reveals Hemingway's carefully controlled habit of understatement. *For Whom The Bell Tolls* is a prose epic of the Spanish people with a message to the whole mankind that war is a bad thing.

REFERENCES

1. Carlos Baker, Hemingway : The Write As Artist (Princeton, N.J.: Princeton University Press, 1963), p. 352.

2. Horst Frenz, ed., Novel Lectures Literature (New York: Elsevier, 1969), p. 497.
3. Carlos Baker, *op.cit.*, p. 237.
4. Baker, p. 147.
5. Horst Frenz, *op.cit.*, p. 502.
6. Carlos Baker, *op.cit.*, p. 287.
7. Baker, p. 241.
8. Horst Frenz, *op. cit.*, p. 499.
9. Frenz, p. 497.
10. Carlos Baker, *op. cit.*, pp. 245-46.
11. Baker, p. 247.
12. Chaman novel, *The Narrative Pattern in Ernest Hemingway's Fiction* (Delhi: Vikas, 1971, p . 21.
13. Carlos Baer, *op. cit.*, p. 249.

Appendix

Glossary of the Spanish Words and Phrases

Salud, Camarada. Greetings, Comrade.

Alpargatas (Sp.). hemp Sandals.

Guardia Civil (Sp.). Civil Guards.

Pauvre Pablo. Poor Pablo.

Hola (Sp.) Woman or wife

Muv flojo (Sp.). Very weak

Matador de toros (Sp.).Bullfighter

Nada (Sp.). Nothing.

Mequina (Sp.). Machine. Here, a machinegun.

Ingles (Sp.). English

Me voy (Sp.) I go.

No es nada (Sp.). It is nothing to worry about

Barracho (Sp.) Drunkard.

Ya lo veo (Sp.). see him now.

Buenas, Comadre (Sp.). Good after noon, friend.

Chico (Colloquials Spanish). Chaap, felow.

la gente (Sp.). The people

Olel (Sp.). Bravol

Oue va (Sp.). Think nothing of it.

Lo sabes? (Sp.). Do you know?

Bueno (Sp.). Good

Oue mas da (Sp.). What does it matter.

Que tal? (Sp.). What does it matter.

Que tal? (Sp.). How is it going?

Pues nada (Sp.). Well, nothing.

Hombre (Sp.). Man.

Tonto (Sp.) Fool.

Como siempre (Sp.). As usual.

Che (Sp.) A form of address, such as, Say! listen?

Vamost (Sp) Come now!

Feria (Sp.). Fair.

Paella (Sp.). Dish of rice with meat, chicken and seafood.

Centimes (Sp.) The hundredth part of a Spanish peseta.

Traca (Sp). A string of firecrackers.

Guapa (Sp.). Beautiful woman.

Vamos a ver (Sp) Let us see.

Virgen (Sp.) Our Lady, the Blessed Virgin Mary.

Novio (Sp.) Fiance.

Desde leugo (Sp.). Of course.

Pero es muy vivo (Sp.). Buthesvery smart.

Sn Picardia (Sp.). Without mischief.

Es muy vivo (Sp.). He is very smart.

Pero, venga (Sp.) But,come here.

Que no? (Sp.) What no?

Civiles (Sp.). Civilians.

Vaya (Sp.) Thank goodness.

Plaza (Sp.). Squace, market place or fortified town.

Cupea (Sp.). Amateur bull-baiting show at the time of a fiesta.

Agua (Sp.) Water.

Cabron (Sp.) Cuckold.

Canalla (Sp.). Scoundrel.

Arriba Espana (sp.). Hrrah Spain!

Buen provecho (Sp.) Good appetite.

A sus ordenes (Sp.) at yur service.

Bota (Sp.). Wineskin.

Es Debate (Sp.). The Debate, A Catholic newspaper.

Viva la Anarquia (Sp.). Long live the Anarchy.

Viva la Liberatad (Sp.). Long live the Liberty.

No hay derecho, mujer (Sp.). Woman, you have no right.

Corrida (Sp.) Bullfight.

NO hace falta (Sp.). It is not needed.

Buena gente (Sp.). The good people

Deja (Sp.). Russian.

Dentro de las gravedad (Sp.). Within the limits of the danger.

Guerrilleros (Sp.). Guerrillas.

Algo raro (sp.) Somewhat rare.

Si, algo raro, pero bueno (Sp.). Yes, a little rare, but good.

Murio (Sp.). He died.

Como fue? (Sp.). How was it?

Menos mal (Sp.) Less bad.

Es muy util (Sp.) It is very useful.

Ya iras, mujer (Sp.). You will go woman.

Por que (Sp.). Why.

Soy muy delicade (Sp.) I am very delicate.

Pues me voy (Sp.). So I am going.

Que beuno (Sp.) That is good

Ahora (Sp.). Now.

Heute (Ger.). Today.

Esta noche (Sp.). Tonight.

Muerto (Sp.). Dead.

Guerra (Sp.). War.

Cherie (Sp.) Dear.

Prenda (Sp.) Dear love.

Pues es muy raro (Sp.). But it is very strange.

Cómo que no. hija? (Sp). Why not, daughter?

Gitanos (Sp.). Gypsies.

A mi que? (Sp.) What do I care?

Que sencillol (Sp.). How simple!

Hola, Viejo (Sp.) Hello, old man.

Viojo (Sp.). Old man.

No se (Sp.). I don't know

Estados Unidos (Sp.) The United States.

Sinverguenza (Sp.).Shamless.

Negro (Sp.). Black

Carbon (Sp.). A man who takes an unfair advantage of a person.

Que te importa (Sp.). This is not your business.

Facciosos (Sp.). Rebels.

Estoy listo (Sp.). I am ready.

Leche (Sp.). Milk

De versa (Sp.). Truly, in earnest.

Muy bien (Sp.) Vey good.

Plaza de Toros (Sp.) Bullring.

Casas de putas (Sp.). Whorehouses.

Como tu (Sp.) Like you.

Ojala no (sp.) I hope not.

Oue caballo mas bonita (Sp.). What a pretty horse!

Oue caballow mas hermoso (Sp.). What a beautifully horse!

Vete (Sp.). Go get out.

Dijamos (Sp.) Leave us (alone).

Hijo de la gran puta! (Sp.). Son of a bitch!

Ah. Mi madre (Ap.). Oh, my mother!

Oue tiol (Sp.) What a man!

Anda! (Sp.) Go!

Pues (Sp.) Why.

Carajo (Sp.) Bastard.

Canalla (Sp.). Well.

Es muy hombre (Sp.) He is man.

Pobre (Sp.). Poor person.

Jodido (Sp.) Spoiled, ruined.

Locos (Sp.). Insane persons.

Ya lo se (Sp.) Already I know it.

Resistir y fortificer es vencer (Sp) To resist and to fortify is to conquer.

Bandidos! (Sp.). Bandits!

Que cosa mas mala es I Guerra (Sp). What a bad thing war is.

Estado (Sp). Coward

Seguridad (Sp.). Police.

Viva la Republica (Sp.). Long live the Republic.

Viva la Republica y vivan mis padres (Sp. Long live the Republic and long live my parents.

Viva (Sp.). Long live.

Muy, muy serio (Sp.) Very, very serious.

Viva la Libertad! (Sp.). Long live the liberty.

Bodega (Sp.). Wineshop.

Tomate (Sp.) Run.

Ompadre (Sp.) Friend.

Dentro de l gravedad (Sp.). considering the (grave) situation.

Ni tu ni dios (Sp.) Neither you, nor God.

Bueno, y que? Sp) Good, so what?

En el fondo no soy cobarde (Sp.) At bottom, I am not a coward.

Listo (Sp.). Ready

Hombre (Sp.) Man.

Buena Suerte (Sp.). Good luck.

Tiene mania de fusilar gente (Sp.). He has a mania for shooting people.

Buena caza (Sp.) Nice hunting.

Sinnovedad (Sp.) Without.

Juve que rematarlo (Sp.). I had to finish him off.

Yo mate uno tambien (Sp.). I killed one too.

Que puta es la Guerra (Sp.) What a whore war is.

Bibliography

Aldrige, John W. *After the Lost Generation: A Critical Study of the writers of the Two Wars*. New York: The Noonday Press, 1963.

Anderson, Charles R. "Hemingway's other Style." *Modern Language Notes,* 76 (1961), 434-442.

Aronowitz, Alfred G. And Peter Hamill. *Ernest Hemingway: The Life and Death of a man*. New York: Lancer Books Inc. 1961.

Asselineau, Roger (ed.). *The Literary Reputation of Hemingway in Europe,* New York: New York Univ. Press, 1965.

Atkins, John, *The Art of Ernest Hemingway: His Work and Personality*, London: Peter Nevill, 1962.

Backman, Melvin. "Hemingway: The Matador and the Crucified, *Modern Fiction Studies,* ((August, 1955), 2-11.

Baker, Carlos. *Ernest Hemingway: A Life Story*. New York: Bantm Books, Incl., 1970 (1969).

———, *Ernest Hemingway: Critiques of Four Major Novels.* New York: Charles Scribner's Sons, 1962.

———, *Hemingway and his Critics: An International Anthology*. New York: Hill and Wang, 1961.

———, *Hemingway: The Writer as Artist*. Princeton: Princeton Univ. Press , 3rd revise[illegible] edition, 1963.

Baker, Sheridan, *Ernest Hemingway: An Introduction and Interpretation*, New York: Barnes and Noble, Inc., 1967.

Balakian, Anna. *The Symbolist Movement: A Critical Appraisal.* New York Random House, 1967.

Barea, Auturo, "Not Spain but Hemingway," *Horizon*, 3 (May, 1941), 350-361.

Beach, Joseph Warren. *American Fiction: 1920-40.* New York: MacMillan, 1941.

............, "How Do You Like It Now, Gentlemen?" *Sewanee Review*, 59 (Spring, 1951), 311-328).

Benson, Jackson J. *Hemingway: The Writers' Art of Self-Defense.* Minneapolis: University of Minnesota Press, 1969.

Bessie, Alvash C. *The Un-Americans.* London: John Calder, 1967.

Bishop, John Peale. "Homage to Hemingway," *The Collected Essays of John Peale Bishop.* New York: Charles Scribner's Sons, 1948.

Brady, Charles A. "Portrait of Hemingway," *Americans*, 105 (July 22, 1951), 546-548.

Brooks, Cleanth. *The Hidden God: Studies in Hemingway,* Faulkner, Yeats, *Eliot and Warren.* New Haven, Conn: Yale Unive. Press, 1963.

Brown, Deming. "Hemingway in Russia," *American Quarterly*, 5 (Summers, 1953), 143-56.

Burhans, Clinton S., Jr., "*The Old Man and The Sea* Hemingway's Tragic Vision of Man.: *American Literature* 31 (1960), 446-55).

Callaghan, Morley. *That Summer in Paris. Memoirs of Tangled Friendships with Hemingway, Fitzgerald, and some others.* New York: Coward McCann, 1963.

Carpenter, Frederic I. "Hemingway Achieves the Fifth Dimension," *PMLA*, 69 (Sept., 1954), 711-18.

Colvert, James B. "Ernest Hemingway's Morality in a Action," *American Literature*, 37 (No. 1965), 372-385.

Connolly, Cyril. Hemingway's Speech, *New Statesman and Nation*, 14 (Oct. 16, 1937), 606.

Cowley, Malcolm, *Exile's Return: A Literary Odyssey of the 1920's*. New York: The Viking Press, 1951.

———. *Introduction to Hemingway*. New York : The Viking Press, 1944.

Daiches, David, "Ernest Hemingway," *College English*, 2 (May, 1941), 725-736.

DeFalco, Joseph, *The Hero in Hemingway's Short Stories*, Pittsburgh, Pa.: University of Pittsburgh Press, 1963.

Deny, Margaret and William H. Gilman (eds.) *The American Writer and the European Tradition*. Minneapolis, 1950.

Feidelson, Charles, *Symbolism and American Literature* Chicago: University of Chicago Press, 1953.

Fenton, Charles A. *The Apprenticeship of Ernest Hemingway*. New York: Farrar, Straus and Young, 1954.

Fiedler, Leslie. *Love an Death in the American Novel*. New York: Criterion Books, 1960.

Frankenberg, Lloyd. "themes and Characters in Hemingway's Latest Period," *Southern Review*, 7 (Spring, 1942), 776-788.

Frenz Horst, (ed.) *Nobel Lectures Literature*. New York: Elsevier, 1969.

Friedman, Norman, "Criticism and the Novel: Hardy, Hemingway, Crane, Woolf, Conrad," *Antioch Review* , 18 (Fall, 1958), 342-70.

Friedrich, Otto. "Ernest Hemingway: Joy Through Strength," *American Scholar*, 26 (Autumn, 1957), 518-530.

Galbraith, S.J.L. *Hemingway's For Whom The Bell Tolls and A Farewell to Arms*, Notes. London: Coles, 1967.

Gannes,Harry and Theodore, Repard. *Spain in Revolt*. New York: Alfred A. Knopf, 1936.

Geismar, Maxwell. *Writers in Crisis: The American Novel: 1925-40*. Boston: Houghton Mifflin Co., 1942.

Gellens, Jay (ed.). "Introduction," *Twentieth Century Interpretations of a Farewell to Arms*. Englewood Cliffs New Jersey: Prentice-Hall,Inc., 1970.

Gorodon, Caroline. "Notes on Hemingway and Kafka," *Sweanee Review*, 57 (Spring, 1949), 214-226).

Grebstein, Sheldon. "Controversy," *American Sholar*, 27 (Spring, 1958), 229, 31.

-------, *Hemingway's Craft*. Corbondale: Southern Illionois University Press, 1972.

Gurko, Leo. "the Achievement of Ernest Hemingway," *English Journal*, 41 (1952), 291-298.

——, *Ernest Hemingway and the Pursuit of Heroism*. New York: Thomas, Y. Cromwell Company, 1968.

Halliday, E.M. "Hemingway's Ambiguity: Symbolism and Irony, "*American Literature*, 28 (1956), 1-22.

Hart, Henry (ed.). *The Writer in a Changing World*. New York: Equinox Cooperative Press, 1937.

Hemingway, Ernest. *Three Stores and Ten Poems*. Paris: Contact Publishing Co., 1923.

———, *The Short Stories of Ernest Hemingway*. New York: Charles Scribner's Sons, 1953. Stories from 1925 to 1953.

———, *The Torrents of Spring*. New York: Charles Scribner's Sons, 1926.

———,*The Sun Also Rises*. New York: Charles Scribner's Sons, 1926.

———, *A Farewell to Arms*. New York : Charles Scribner's Sons, 1929.

———, *Death in the Afternoon*, New York: Charles Scribner's Sons, 1932.

———,*Green Hills of Africa*. New York : Chares Scriber's Sons, 1935.

———,*To Have and Have not*. New York: Charles Scribner's Sons, 1937.

———,*The Spanish Earth*. New York: Charles Scribner's Sons, 1938.

———,*The Fifth Column*, New York: Charles Scribner's Sons, 1940, 1938.

———,*For Whom the Bell Tolls*. New York: Charles Scribner's Sons, 1940.

———,*Men at War*. New York: Crown Publishers, 1942.

———,*Across the River and into the Trees*. New York: Charles Scribner's Sons, 1950.

———,*The Old Man and the Sea*. New York: Charles Scribner's Sons, 1952.

———,*A Moveable Feast*. New York: Charles Scribner's Sons, 1964.

———,*By-Line: Ernest Hemingway*. New York : Charles Scribner's Sons, 1967.

———,*Islands in the Streams*. New York: Charles Scribner's Sons, 1970.

———,*The Nick Adams Stories*. New York: Charles Scribner's Sons, 1962.

Hotchner, A.E. Pana Hemingway, New York: A Bantam Book, 1967.

Hovey Richard B. *Hemingway: The Inward Terrain*. Seattle: University of Washington Press, 1968.

Isbelle, Julianne, *Hemingway's Religious Experience*. New York Vantage Press, 1954.

Jackson, Gabriel, The *Spanish Republican and the Civil War: 1931-39*. Princeton, New Jersey: Princeton University Press, 1965.

Kazin, Alfred. *On Native Grounds: An Interpretation of Modern American Literature*. New York: Harcourt, Brace, 1942.

Killinger, John. *Hemingway and the Dead Gods*. Kentucky: University of Kentucky Press, 1960.

Lama, Leo. *Hemingway: A Pictorial Biography*. New York: The Viking Press, 1961.

Levin, Harry, "Observation on the style of Ernest Hemingway," *Kenyon Review*, 13 (Autumn, 1941), 581-609.

Lewis, Robert W. Jr. *Hemingway on Love*. Austin: University of Texas Press, 1965.

Lewis, Wyndham. "The Dumb Ox: A Study of Ernest Hemingway," men Without Art London, 1934.

Luccock, Halford E. Contemporary American Literature and Religion. Chicago: Willet-Clark, 1934.

Manning, Robert, "Hemingway in Cuba," *Atlantic Monthly*, 216 (August, 1965), 101-108.

McCaffery, John K. (ed.). *Ernest Hemingway: The Man and His Work Cleveland*; 1950.

Moloney, Michael F. "Ernest Hemingway: The Missing Thrid Dimension," *Fifty Years of the American Novel*. Harold C. Gardiner, ed. New York: Charles Scribner's Sons, 1952.

Montgomery, Constance Cappel. *Hemingway in Michigan*. New York: Fleet Publishing Corporation, 1966,

Muste, John M. *Say That We Saw Spain Die: Literary Consequences of Spanish Civil War*. Scattle: University of Washington Press, 1966.

Nahal, Chaman, *The Narrative Pattern in Ernest Hemingway's*

Fiction Rutherford, New Jersey: Fairleigh Dickinson Univ. Press, 1971.

Peterson, Richard K. *Hemingway: Direct and Oblique*. The Hague: Moulton, 1969.

Plimpton, George, "Ernest Hemingway," Paris Review, 18 (Spring, 1958, 61-82.

Ross, *Lillian Portrait of Hemingway*. New York: Simon and Schuster, 1950.

Rovit, Earl. *Ernest Hemingway*. New York: Twyne Publishers. Inc., 1963.

Samuels. *Lee A Hemingway Check List*, New York: Charles Scribner's Sons, 1951.

Sanders, David. "Ernest Hemingway's Spanish Civil War Experience," *American Quarterly*, 12 (1960), 133-143.

Sanderson, S.F. *Ernest Hemingway*. Edingurgh: Oliver and Boyd, 1961.

Sanford, Marcelline *Hemingway. At the Hemingways: A Family Portrait*. Boston: Atlantic-Little, Brown, 1962.

Savage, D.S. *The Withered Branch: Six Studies in the Modern Novel*. London: Eyre and Spottiswoode, Ltd., 1950.

Schorer, Mark. "The Background of a Style," *Kenyon Review*, 3 (Winter, 1941), 101-105.

———,"*With Grace Under Pressure*," New Republic, 127 (Oct. 6, 1952), 19-20.

Shapiro, Charles (ed.). *Twelve Original Essays on Great American Novels*. Detroit: Wayne State University Press, 1958.

Shaw, Samuel. *Ernest Hemingway*. New York: Frederick Unger Publishing Company, 1973.

Singer, Kurt. *Hemingway: Life and Death of a Giant*. Los Angeles: Holloway House, 1961.

Srivastava, Ramesh. *Hemingway and His For Whom The Bell Tolls*. Amritsar: Guru Nanak Dev University, 1980.

Thomas, *Hugh The Spanish Civil War*. New York: Harper and Brothers, 1961.

Thorp, Willard . *American Writing in the Twentieth Century*. Cambridge, Mass: Harvard University Press, 1963.

Waldhorn, *Arthur: A Reader's Guide to Ernest Hemingway*. New York: Farrar, Straus an Girous, 1972.

———,(ed.) *Ernest Hemingway: A Collection of Criticism*. New York: McGraw-Hill Book Company, 1973.

Watts, Emily Stipes. *Ernest Hemingway and the Arts*. Chicago: University of Illinois Press, 1971.

Weeks, Robert P. (Ed.) *Hemingway: A Collection of Critical Essays*. Englewood Cliffs, New Jersey: Prentice-Hall, Inc., 1962.

West Ray B., Jr. "Ernest Hemingway: Death in the Evening," *Antioch Review*, 4 (1944), 569, 80.

Wilson, Edmund. "Hemingway: Gauge of Morale," *The Wound and the Bow*. The New York: Oxford Unive. Press, 1947.

Wylder, Delbert E. *Hemingway's Heroes*. Albuquerque Univ. of new Mexico Press, 1969.

Wyrick, Green D. *The World of Hemingway: A Critical Study*. The Emporia. State Research Studies, 11, No. 1 (1953).

Young, Philip. *Ernest Hemingway: A Reconsideration*. Revised Edition. New York: Harcourt, Brace and World Inc., 1966.

———,, and Charles W. Mann (edrs.), *The Hemingway Manuscripts : An Inventory*. University Part: The Pennsylvania State Univ. Press, 1969.

Index